Foods from the Farm

by Rebecca Weber

Content Advisers: MeeCee Baker, Ph.D.,
Assistant Professor, College of Education,
Department of Curriculum and Instruction,
The Pennsylvania State University

Robert E. Mikesell, Ph.D., Senior Extension Associate,
The Department of Dairy and Animal Sciences,
The Pennsylvania State University

Reading Adviser: Rosemary G. Palmer, Ph.D.,
Department of Literacy, College of Education,
Boise State University

Spyglass
BOOKS

COMPASS POINT BOOKS

Minneapolis, Minnesota

Compass Point Books
3109 West 50th Street, #115
Minneapolis, MN 55410

Visit Compass Point Books on the Internet at *www.compasspointbooks.com*
or e-mail your request to *custserv@compasspointbooks.com*

Photographs ©: Jose Luis Pelaez, Inc./Corbis, cover; Corbis, 4, 14, 17; John Elk III, 5 (top), 7;
Image Library, 5 (bottom), 10 (right); PhotoDisc, 6, 18; USDA/ARS/Ken Hammond, 9, 13, 15, 19;
USDA/ARS/Joe Valbuena, 8; Comstock, 10 (left), 11, 16; Unicorn Stock Photos/Eric R. Berndt, 12.

Editor: Patricia Stockland
Photo Researcher: Marcie C. Spence
Designer: Jaime Martens

Library of Congress Cataloging-in-Publication Data
Weber, Rebecca.
  Foods from the farm / by Rebecca Weber.
    p. cm. — (Spyglass books)
  Summary: Describes different foods and products that come from farms, including dairy,
  grains, poultry, meat, and household items.
  ISBN 0-7565-0624-7 (hardcover)
  1. Food—Juvenile literature. 2. Farm produce—Juvenile literature.
  [1. Farm produce. 2. Food crops.] I. Title. II. Series.
  TX355.W385 2004
  641.3—dc22   2003014479

Contents

To Your Table. 4

Meat. 6

Milk and Eggs. 10

Fruits and Vegetables. . . .14

Set the Table. 18

Fun Farm Facts. 20

Glossary. 22

Learn More. 23

Index. 24

NOTE: Glossary words are in **bold** the first time they appear.

To Your Table

Almost everything you eat comes from a farm. There are different kinds of farms.

A Sugar Farm

Did you know sugar comes from farms? People can get sugar from sugar cane or sugar beets.

Meat

Most meat comes
from farms.

Beef, pork, and poultry
all come from animals.
These animals live on farms.

The farm animals get big. They go to a meat *packer.* There, they are *slaughtered.* Their meat is cut and put into packages. Then people buy the meat in a store.

Hard Work

Butchers are people who cut and sell meat. Some butchers work in their own shops. Other butchers work in packing plants or grocery stores.

Fish Farms

Some fish are raised in special water farms. Baby fish called fry hatch from eggs. Then they live in ponds. People feed the fish until they are large.

9

Milk and Eggs

Milk and eggs come from farms.

Milk comes from cows and goats. Chickens lay eggs.

Good and Healthy

Milk is full of *protein* and *vitamins.*
These help people grow strong
and healthy.

Milk goes to a factory.
Some milk is put into bottles.
Other milk becomes cheese,
yogurt, butter, and ice cream.

Farmers put eggs in
special *cartons.* Then they
send them to the store.

Busy Cow!

One cow can give 200,000 glasses of milk in its lifetime.

Fruits and Vegetables

Fruits and vegetables come from farms.

Fruits such as apples grow in *orchards.* Vegetables such as lettuce grow in fields.

People *harvest* the fruits and vegetables. Some are sent to grocery stores. Others go to factories. There they are canned, frozen, or used to make other foods.

Did You Know?

Wheat is grown on a farm. Wheat flour is used to make bread. That means bread comes from a farm, too.

Healthy Land, Healthy Food

Many farmers plant a different *crop* each year. This keeps the plants healthy so they grow more food.

Set the Table

Many other goods come from farms.

Cotton grows on a farm. The cloth in a napkin comes from cotton plants.

Warm and Woolly

The wool in your sweater is from a farm, too. It was *sheared* from a sheep. Many things come from the farm!

Fun Farm Facts

- The United States has more than 2 million farms.

- Pigs cannot sweat when they get hot. Some farmers spray them with sprinklers to keep them cool.

- The first carrots grown on a farm were white, purple, and yellow.

- Pumpkins and squash are fruits, not vegetables.

- Soybeans are an amazing crop. They can be eaten as a healthy food. They can also be used to make paint and plastic!

Glossary

carton–a kind of box

crop–a plant that is grown to be eaten or used in other ways

harvest–to pick for eating

orchards–fields of trees that grow fruit

packer–a person or company that processes meat

protein–part of food that helps build and repair the body

sheared–clipped, cut, or trimmed

slaughtered–killed for food

vitamins–parts of food that help your body grow and work

Learn More

Books

Patent, Dorothy Hinshaw. *Where Food Comes From.* New York: Holiday House, 1991.

Spilsbury, Louise. *Rice.* Chicago: Heinemann Library, 2001.

On the Web

For more information on Foods from the Farm, use FactHound to track down Web sites related to this book.

1. Go to *www.compasspointbooks.com/facthound*
2. Type in this book ID: 0756506247
3. Click on the *Fetch It* button. Your trusty FactHound will fetch the best Web sites for you!

23

Index

animals, 6, *6*, 7, *7*, 10, *12*, 13, *13*, 19, *19*
beef, 6
bread, 16, *16*
butter, 12
cheese, *10*, 12
chickens, *6*, 10
cotton, 18, *18*
cows, 10, *12*, 13, *13*
eggs, 10, 12
farms, *4, 5, 6, 9, 14, 17*

fruits, 14, *14*, 15, *15*
ice cream, 12
meat, 6–7, 8, *8*
milk, 10, *10*, 11–13, *11, 12*
pork, 6
poultry, 6, *6*, 10
sheep, 19, *19*
sugar cane, 5, *5*
vegetables, 14, 15
wheat, 16
wool, 19, *19*
yogurt, 12

GR: J
Word Count: 178

From Rebecca Weber

The world is such a great place! I love teaching kids how to take care of themselves and take care of nature.

24